Questions and Answers: Countries

Indonesia

A Question and Answer Book

by Mary Dodson Wade

Consultant:
Astari M. Daenuy
Program Officer
The United States-Indonesia Society

Capstone
press®

Mankato, Minnesota

Fact Finders is published by Capstone Press
151 Good Counsel Drive, P.O. Box 669, Mankato, Minnesota 56002.
www.capstonepress.com

Library of Congress Cataloging-in-Publication Data
Wade, Mary Dodson.
    Indonesia: a question and answer book / by Mary Dodson Wade; consultant,
    Astari M. Daenuy.
    p. cm. —(Fact finders. Questions and answers. Countries)
    Includes bibliographical references (p. 31) and index.
    Summary: "Describes the geography, history, economy, and culture of Indonesia in a
question–and–answer format"—Provided by publisher.
    Includes bibliographical references and index.
    ISBN–13: 978–0–7368–6409–1 (hardcover)
    ISBN–10: 0–7368–6409–1 (hardcover)
    1. Indonesia—Miscellanea—Juvenile literature. I. Title. II. Series.
DS615.W324 2007
959.8—dc22   2006005055

Editorial Credits
Silver Editions, editorial, design, and production; Kia Adams, set designer; Ortelius Design,
    Inc., cartographer; Jo Miller, photo researcher; Scott Thoms, photo editor

Photo Credits
Art Directors/Joan Wakelin, 15; Art Directors/Peter Stagg, cover (foreground); Corbis/
Dean Conger, 25; Corbis/Jack Fields, 6; Corel, 21, 23, 27; Getty Images Inc./AFP, 7; Getty
Images Inc./AFP/Bay Ismoyo, 19; Getty Images Inc./Dimas Ardian, 9; Getty Images Inc./
Iconica/Diehm, 4; Getty Images Inc./Jonathan Ferrey, 18; Index Stock Imagery/David
Ball, cover (background); Ivan Susanto, 17; Michele Burgess, 20, 24; One Mile Up, Inc., 29
(flag); Peter Arnold, Inc./BIOS, 1; Peter Arnold, Inc./Julio Etchart, 16; Photodisc, 8; Richard
Sutherland, 29; Victor Englebert, 11; Wolfgang Kaehler, 12; Zuma Press/eyewire/Peter
Bennett, 13

1 2 3 4 5 6 11 10 09 08 07 06

Table of Contents

Where is Indonesia? 4

When did Indonesia become a country? 6

What type of government does Indonesia have? 8

What kind of housing does Indonesia have? 10

What are Indonesia's forms of transportation? 12

What are Indonesia's major industries? 14

What is school like in Indonesia? 16

What are Indonesia's favorite sports and games? 18

What are the traditional art forms in Indonesia? 20

What holidays do Indonesians celebrate? 22

What are the traditional foods of Indonesia? 24

What is family life like in Indonesia? 26

Features

Indonesia Fast Facts 28

Money and Flag 29

Learn to Speak Bahasa Indonesia 30

Glossary 30

Internet Sites 31

Read More 31

Index 32

Where is Indonesia?

Indonesia is a string of 17,508 islands in the Pacific Ocean. They stretch 3,000 miles (4,800 kilometers) from Southeast Asia to Australia. The distance is about the same as from New York City to Los Angeles.

People live on 6,000 of the islands. About half the country's population lives on Java.

Mount Bromo, in East Java, is one of Indonesia's many active volcanoes.

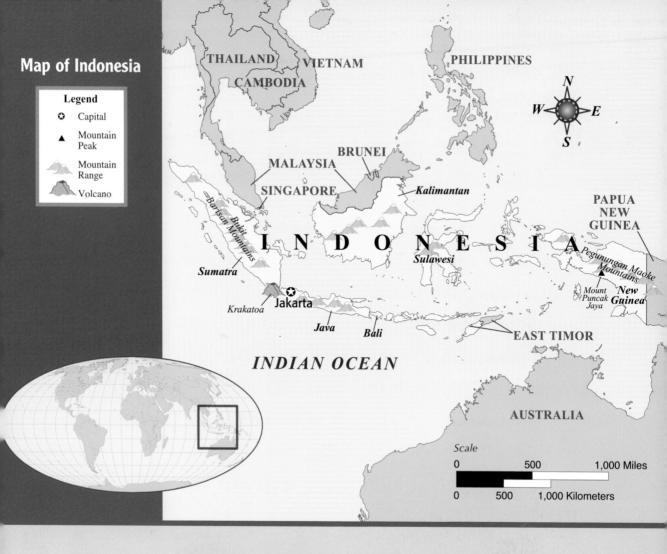

Map of Indonesia

Legend
- ✪ Capital
- ▲ Mountain Peak
- Mountain Range
- Volcano

THAILAND VIETNAM PHILIPPINES

CAMBODIA

N
W E
S

BRUNEI

MALAYSIA

SINGAPORE Kalimantan

PAPUA NEW GUINEA

Barisan Mountains

Bukit

I N D O N E S I A

Pegunungan Maoke Mountains

Sumatra

Sulawesi

Mount Puncak Jaya New Guinea

Krakatoa Jakarta

Java Bali

EAST TIMOR

INDIAN OCEAN

AUSTRALIA

Scale
0   500   1,000 Miles
0   500   1,000 Kilometers

Indonesia is part of the Pacific Ring of Fire, the area where volcanoes and earthquakes occur at the edge of the ocean. In December 2004, an undersea earthquake caused a **tsunami** that killed more than 150,000 people in Indonesia.

When did Indonesia become a country?

Indonesia became an independent country in 1945, but people have lived there for thousands of years. About 2,000 years ago, small tribes began to form independent kingdoms. The last great kingdom, the Majapahit Empire, lasted over 200 years.

The Portuguese arrived in Indonesia in 1511. They began to rule Indonesia. The Portuguese traded Indonesian spices to the rest of Europe.

Fact!

Indonesia has many cultures. Its official motto is "Unity in Diversity."

Achmed Sukarno demanded independence for the Indonesian people.

In the 1600s, the Dutch took over the spice trade and began to rule Indonesia. The Dutch lost control of Indonesia to Japan in World War II (1939–1945). After the war, a local leader named Achmed Sukarno became Indonesia's first president.

What type of government does Indonesia have?

Indonesia is a **republic**. People vote for a president and a vice president every five years. All citizens 17 years of age or older may vote. People who are married may vote even if they are younger than 17.

Fact!

Since its independence 60 years ago, Indonesia has had only six presidents.

A woman votes in Jakarta in the 2004 election for president.

Every five years, Indonesians also vote for members of the legislature. Indonesia has a national legislature called the People's Consultative Assembly. It meets at least once a year in Indonesia's capital, Jakarta.

What kind of housing does Indonesia have?

Homes in Indonesia vary. Wealthy people live in stone or **stucco** houses with modern conveniences. In poor areas, houses may not have running water.

People in rural areas often build their houses of wood. Wood is cheap because Indonesia has many forests.

Where do people live in Indonesia?

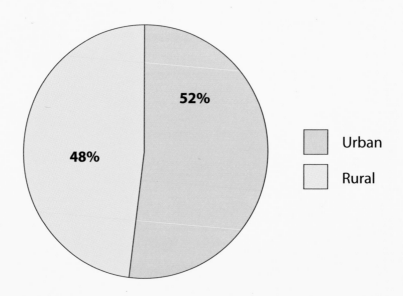

52%

48%

Urban

Rural

These houses are built on wooden piers that lift them above ground. This protects them from flooding caused by heavy rains.

Nearly half of all Indonesians live on Java. Java is slightly smaller than the U.S. state of Louisiana. Most people on Java live in single-family houses.

In West Sumatra and South Sulawesi, people build **traditional** houses. They are made of wood with **thatched** roofs.

What are Indonesia's forms of transportation?

Traditionally, Indonesians used boats to go from island to island. The *pinisi* is a traditional boat that is still being used. Today, airplanes provide quick transportation between islands and to other countries.

City streets are choked with cars, trucks, and motorbikes. It is not unusual to see a motorbike weaving through traffic carrying a father, mother, and two children.

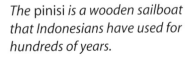

The pinisi *is a wooden sailboat that Indonesians have used for hundreds of years.*

Cars, vans, motorcycles, and carriages all travel the busy streets of Jakarta.

Instead of a bus, some people ride in a three-wheeled taxicab called a *becak*. Others might ride in a minibus called an *opelet*. People can even hire a motorcycle taxi called an *ojék*.

What are Indonesia's major industries?

Indonesia has resources other countries need. It **exports** more natural gas than any other country in the world. Indonesia also produces crude oil and copper.

Manufacturing is also important in Indonesia. Textiles, cement, chemical fertilizers, wood products, and beautiful carved furniture are all manufactured in Indonesia.

What does Indonesia import and export?

Imports	Exports
chemicals	chocolate
foodstuffs	electrical appliances
fuels	natural gas
machinery	plywood
equipment	rubber
	textiles

A man on a plantation in Sumatra taps a tree for rubber.

Farmers in Indonesia harvest rice, cassava, peanuts, cocoa, rubber, palm oil, and spices for export. Indonesia is the world's third largest producer of chocolate.

Tourism is also an important industry in Indonesia. The Temple of Borobudur in Java is the largest Buddhist temple in the world.

What is school like in Indonesia?

Education is important to Indonesians. Students enter kindergarten at age 5 and spend six years in primary school. This is followed by three years in junior high school and three years in high school. Some then go to a university.

School starts in July. Students get breaks for several religious holidays throughout the school year.

Fact!

Almost 90 percent of Indonesians can read and write.

Private schools, like this one in Sumatra, follow their own uniform code.

Parents buy uniforms and books for their children. In public schools, uniforms differ for each grade level. Children in elementary school wear white shirts with red shorts or skirts. In junior high, students wear white shirts with navy blue shorts or skirts. High school students wear white shirts with gray pants or skirts.

What are Indonesia's favorite sports and games?

Soccer and badminton are national sports in Indonesia. Indonesia won gold and bronze medals in men's badminton in the 2004 Olympics.

In villages, people enjoy playing volleyball. Indonesians also enjoy a unique Southeast Asian game called *sepak takraw.* It is a cross between volleyball and soccer. A player's hand touches the ball only when serving. The rest of the time players use only their feet.

Fact!

Taufik Hidayat won an Olympic gold medal in 2004 for men's singles badminton.

Boosak Ponsana plays at the Indonesian Open Badminton tournament in September 2005.

One ancient sport enjoyed in Indonesia is martial arts. Indonesian martial arts is called *pencak silat*. There are many different positions and movements that use hands, elbows, knees, and feet. Demonstrations of *pencak silat* can be seen today at traditional weddings and festivals.

What are the traditional art forms in Indonesia?

Indonesia is famous for batik cloth. Wax on the cloth separates the colors as the cloth is dyed. Then the wax is boiled away.

Indonesia is also known for its shadow puppets. *Wayang kulit* puppets are flat leather puppets. *Wayang golek* are rod puppets that look like dolls. People use these puppets to act out Hindu stories.

Fact!

Classical dance is an important art form in Indonesia. Some children begin taking lessons as young as age 6.

Metallophones are one of the instruments played in Gamelan orchestras.

Gamelan music is a tradition in Indonesia. A Gamelan orchestra makes soothing music with drums, xylophones, and large gongs. A complete orchestra may have up to 80 instruments.

What holidays do Indonesians celebrate?

Indonesia has many holidays because it has many cultures. Often these holidays are religious celebrations. Muslims observe the month of Ramadan. At the end of Ramadan, they celebrate Eid al-Fitr with presents and food. Buddhists celebrate Buddha's birthday in spring. Christians celebrate Christmas and Easter.

What other holidays do people in Indonesia celebrate?

Ascension of Christ into Heaven
Bali's Day of Absolute Silence
Islamic New Year
Muhammad's Birthday
National Education Day

Young drummers march in an Independence Day parade.

Indonesians observe New Year's Day on January 1, just as Americans do. But they also celebrate *Imlek*, or Chinese New Year. Indonesia's national holiday is Independence Day, celebrated on August 17. Schools and businesses close for this holiday.

What are the traditional foods of Indonesia?

Almost any meal in Indonesia will include some form of rice, along with coconut and peanuts used in different ways. Coconut milk is used in soups and desserts. Peanuts are mixed with vegetables, and spicy peanut sauce is served with vegetables or steamed rice.

Fact!

Durian is a sweet-tasting fruit that smells so bad many hotels won't let guests bring it in.

Family and friends gather to enjoy a buffet meal in Jogjakarta, Jakarta.

Indonesians eat chicken, beef, seafood, and sometimes pork. *Sate* is a skewer of meat with peanut sauce.

Indonesia has an abundance of fruit. Apples, guava, bananas, and papaya are available year round.

What is family life like in Indonesia?

Indonesian families today are small. There are usually two or three children. The traditions of a particular area often determine how families live.

Javanese people make up 45 percent of Indonesia's population. Their society requires everyone to be well-mannered.

What are the ethnic backgrounds of people in Indonesia?

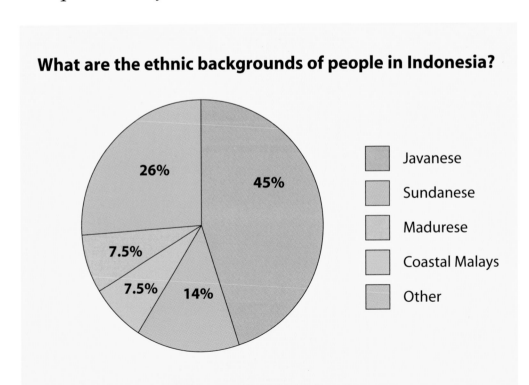

- Javanese
- Sundanese
- Madurese
- Coastal Malays
- Other

This couple, from South Sulawesi, wears traditional clothing for their wedding.

Indonesia is very traditional. Family values and religion are important. Most people follow the Pancasila or Five Pillars, set forth by Sukarno, the first president. These actions are belief in one god, being kind to others, national pride and unity, democratic government, and justice.

Indonesia Fast Facts

Official name:

Republic of Indonesia; Formerly called Netherlands East Indies or Dutch East Indies

Land area:

705,192 square miles of land (1,826,440 square kilometers)

Average annual precipitation (Jakarta):

79 inches (200 centimeters)

Average January temperature (Jakarta):

79 degrees Fahrenheit (26 degrees Celsius)

Average July temperature:

80 degrees Fahrenheit (27 degrees Celsius)

Population:

241,973,879

Capital city:

Jakarta

Languages:

Bahasa Indonesia and local dialects

Natural resources:

petroleum, natural gas, timber, tin

Religions:

Islamic	*88%*
Christian	*8%*
Hindu	*2%*
Buddhist	*1%*
Other, including animist	*1%*

Money and Flag

Money:

Indonesia's money is called the rupiah. The paper money comes in numbers as large as 100,000 rupiahs. In February 2006, one U.S. dollar equaled 9,100 rupiahs. One Canadian dollar equaled about 8,000 rupiahs.

Flag:

The Indonesian flag is very simple. There are two solid bars. The upper bar is red, and the lower bar is white. The design is based on a 13th century Java empire flag. The flag's red color is a symbol for bravery and the white is a symbol of virtue.

Learn to Speak Bahasa Indonesia

Most people in Indonesia speak Bahasa Indonesia. Learn to speak some Bahasa Indonesia words using the chart below.

English	Bahasa Indonesia	Pronunciation
good morning	Selamat pagi	SLAH-maht PAH-ghee
good-bye to a person as you leave	Selamat tinggal	SLAH-maht TING-gahl
good-bye to the person leaving	Selamat jalan	SLAH-maht JAH-lahn
please	Tolong	TOH-long
thank you	Terima Kasih	TREE-mah KAH-see
yes	Ya	YAH
no	Tidak	TEE-dahk

Glossary

export (EKS-port)—to send and sell goods to other countries

republic (ree-PUHB-lik)—a government headed by a president with officials elected by the people

stucco (STUK-oh)—a material made of water, cement, sand, and limestone used to cover homes

thatch (THACH)—a covering for houses made from straw or grass

tourism (TOOR-iz-um)—the business of providing entertainment, food, and lodging for travelers

traditional (truh-DISH-uh-nuhl)—using the styles, manners, and ways of the past

tsunami (tsoo-NAH-mee)—a very large wave caused by an underwater earthquake or volcano

Internet Sites

FactHound offers a safe, fun way to find Internet sites related to this book. All of the sites on FactHound have been researched by our staff.

Here's how:
1. Visit *www.facthound.com*
2. Choose your grade level.
3. Type in this book ID **0736864091** for age-appropriate sites. You may also browse subjects by clicking on letters, or by clicking on pictures and words.
4. Click on the **Fetch It** button.

FactHound will fetch the best sites for you!

Read More

Adamson, Thomas K. *Tsunamis*. Bridgestone Books. Mankato, Minn.: Capstone Press, 2006.

Doak, Robin S. *Indonesia*. First Reports. Minneapolis: Compass Point Books, 2004.

Lim, Robin. *A Ticket to Indonesia*. Minneapolis: Lerner Publishing, 2001.

Weitzman, David. *Rama and Sita: A Tale from Ancient Java*. Boston: David R. Godine, 2002.

Index

agriculture, 15
art forms, 20–21

capital. See Jakarta
climate, 28

education, 16–17
ethnic groups, 26
exports, 14

family life, 26–27
farming. See agriculture
Five Pillars. See Pancasila
flag, 29
food, 14, 24–25

games, 18–19
government, 8–9

Hidayat, Taufik, 18
holidays, 16, 22–23
housing, 10–11

imports, 14
independence, 6
industries, 14–15

Jakarta, 9, 13, 28
Java, 4, 11, 15, 29

landforms, 4–5
language, 28, 30

money, 29
music, 21

natural resources, 28

Pacific Ring of Fire, 5
Pancasila, 27
People's Consultative Assembly, 9
population, 4, 26, 28

religion, 15, 22, 27, 28

schools. See education
sports, 18–19
Sukarno, Achmed, 7, 27
Sulawesi, 11, 27
Sumatra, 11, 15

transportation, 12–13
tsunami, 5

volcanoes, 4, 5

weather. See climate
World War II, 7